LETTERS TO BILL

A Journal of Life, Love, Hope & Friendship

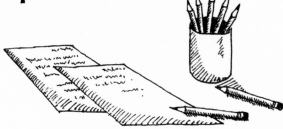

From: John C.

LETTERS TO BILL

by John Christian

Published by Creative Book Printing
Stone Mountain Georgia

ISBN 978-937118-08-2

2012© FIRST EDITION

Printed in USA by
Creative Book Publishing
a company of Budget Transfer Printing & Bindery
www.budgettransfer.com

For more information or to reorder contact
Creative Book Printing
www.budgettransfer.com
creativebook112@aol.com
678.689.0123 • 888.651.8074

IN MEMORY

BILL DARLEY

NOVEMBER 10, 1944-APRIL 19, 2011

William Crawford Darley, Jr. (Bill) grew up in the small south Georgia town of Pelham, Georgia. He graduated from Georgia Institute of Technology with a degree in Industrial Engineering and from Georgia State University with a Masters in Business Administration. After college and his marriage to Glenda Whelchel, he served two years as a lieutenant in the U. S. Army. One of those years, he served as a cargo officer at Newport, Viet Nam.

Bill spent most of his career working for the GA Tech Research Institute doing technical assistance and economic development projects throughout the state of Georgia. During that time he lived in Rome, GA with his family that included two sons. He retired from GA Tech after thirty two years of service.

The things in life that were most important to him were his faith in God, his family (of course his black lab, Smokey, is included as family), his many friends, the great outdoors and nature, hiking, hunting, water sports and woodworking. He was always one who enjoyed life to the fullest, had the highest degree of integrity and was known for his honest and vocal opinions.

He and Glenda came to live at Longleaf at Callaway in Pine Mountain, Georgia after Bill's retirement in 2005. The last years of his life were filled with laughter and hugs from five small grandchildren, chair naps and quiet times at home with Glenda, walks around Longleaf and Callaway Gardens with his dog Smokey, travel to new and revisited destinations, helping care for aging family members, volunteering at Callaway Gardens with the trails crew, and enjoying conversation and good times with friends.

What a lifetime of wonderful memories he left all who knew and loved him!!

INTRODUCTION

This collection of letters is a gift of love and devotion from a wonderful friend and neighbor, John Christian, to my husband, Bill Darley. On February 3, 2010, I had just returned from a trip to South America when Bill informed me he had an MRI scheduled for the next day. His doctor had ordered the test during a regular physical because of some vague symptoms Bill had been having for several weeks. The MRI revealed a tumor in the right thalamus of the brain. A biopsy was performed on February 19, 2010. The diagnosis was not good--an astrocytoma, grade 3--a fast growing, inoperable, malignant brain tumor.

The day Bill had the brain biopsy is the day he began receiving a letter each day from John. John told Bill he would receive a letter each day until he was well. The pages in this book are exactly as John wrote and illustrated them. Some letters are short, some are longer: some are funny, some are spiritual; some are quotes from other people, and some are personal, heartfelt words from John himself. All are thought provoking.

Bill looked forward each day to receiving a new letter, usually accompanied by a visit from his good friend, John. After reading several of the letters, Bill told John, "John, you are writing my funeral!" He would repeat these words often during the next sixteen months.

True to his word, John continued writing and delivering letters. He changed the frequency of the letters in October to once a week instead of daily, but the letters kept coming. They never stopped until Bill left us here on earth and went to be with our Lord and Savior on April 19, 2011. In heaven there is no disease, no discomfort, only total wellness, joy and peace.

As Bill requested, a selection from these letters were read at Bill's memorial service on April 30, 2011.

Glenda Darley
December, 2011

FOREWORD

My dear friend, Bill had brain cancer. I didn't know what to do or say. I ended up saying I'm so sorry, then placed my hand on his shoulder, and told him I would pray for him. But my typical, ordinary response seemed shallow. As I looked into his eyes, I sensed that he was grappling with fear of the unknown (procedures, tests, pain, life, the possibility of death) while also sending me a message to "do something!" I felt awkward. I was at a loss…

Later that day, while in my study at home, the full impact of what my friend was going through clobbered me. I was devastated. I had to take some kind of action. I was looking for a special way to relate to Bill, not realizing that I was also looking for a way to reduce pressure on myself, for I was troubled and was suffering too. During time of prayer, I received inspiration to write Bill a short, five minute letter <u>daily</u>, until he got well. I started thinking… over my lifetime and especially within the last twenty years, I have kept journals. My journals contained prayers, scriptures, stories, thoughts, poems, jokes, even quotes from car bumper stickers. They provided me with excellent resource material to use as I'd write "Letters to Bill."

Each morning during "quiet time," as I prayed for family, friends, situations, I would reach for a sheet of paper and write a short letter to Bill. I had no idea I would end up writing 269 letters. My hope was that the letters would provide encouragement to Bill, but after a while I realized that the process also provided the extra strength I needed to keep me going.

Bill and Smokey

As Bill went through numerous chemo and radiation treatments, through good, medium and bad days, he received great love, prayers, assistance, and encouragement from his wife, Glenda, from his family, and from his friends. We shared good times, had lots of laughs, traveled some, and often walked together through the woods with Bill's black lab, "Smokey."

I feel my letters made a small contribution to Bill's well-being - just one input among many, so graciously given by those who loved him. All of us (church, family, and community) walked together through this long and painful process. As the cancer grew worse and Bill knew he was dying, I had a troubling concern that one day, I would deliver a letter to Bill and he would say, "Enough with the letters - I'm tired of the letters!" but he didn't. He humbly and gratefully accepted each one and often with eyes closed, listened as Glenda or I gently read to him.

I delivered the last letter late in the afternoon of April 19, 2011.

Bill went to be with the Lord at 10:30 that night.

At first, Bill was just my friend, *later he became my brother*.

John Christian

BILL DARLEY--THINGS WE HAVE LEARNED

by Darby Darley, loving daughter-in-law

June, 2011

Don't be concerned with image - Be yourself at all times
Stand up for yourself and for those you love
Have an infectious laugh
Relish time with family
Look forward to a good meal with great anticipation
Spoil your dog
Rest when you are tired - chair naps work well
Visit with friends regularly
Appreciate the sport of people watching
Talk to strangers
Be able to laugh about getting older
Have hobbies
Enjoy time spent outside
Ask for a discount
Work hard; carry a sweat rag if needed
Don't be ashamed to look for "treasures" in someone else's trash
Enjoy getting a "good deal" when shopping
Treasure the time spent holding a baby
Value your family and tell them that you love them

Blessed is the man whose strength is in the Lord
Psalm 84:5

A Note from the Publisher:

Be assured that your book is complete even though a letter number may be missing or a date may be skipped. And there are some letter numbers and dates duplicated.

Remember, this was all written unedited, unscripted and spontaneous. All of the drawings were done by John as he penned the letter. Each letter was given to Bill as it was written so sometimes things got out of sync.

This printing is an exact replica of the original document, maintained in a three ring binder and held close to Glenda's heart. We all hope it will give you comfort, inspiration and peace.

Friday, Feb 19, 2010

Letter # 1

Dear Bill,

This morning at 7:30 am
22 members of Longleaf met
in the Post Office and prayed
for you and Glenda. Countless
others prayed in their homes.

— We prayed for a miracle —

Bill, Keep these letters in a
3 ring binder. You'll receive
one each day until you are well.

From your friend, John

← Gee, they are even 3 hole punched
...ready to go!

Saturday, Feb 20, 2010

Letter # 2

Dear Bill,

So, you have cancer... what's the big deal? Millions have had cancer before you and millions no doubt probably have it right now...

What Cancer Cannot Do

It cannot criple love.
It cannot shatter hope.
It cannot corrode faith.
It cannot destroy peace.
It cannot kill friendships.
It cannot suppress memories.
It cannot silence courage.
It cannot invade the soul.
It cannot steal eternal life.
It cannot conquer the spirit.
.....unless you let it....

— Praying for you daily ! —

From your friend, John

Sunday, Feb 21, 2010

Letter #3

Dear Bill,

We prayed for you & Glenda in
Sunday School and Church

Everyone cares for you both --- _deeply_!

We saw you at the hospital yesterday,
Saturday. You looked good. I saw some
optimism and hope. You had a sense
of humor. You said you couldn't wait 'til
they removed the catheter so you could
take a good pee.

Get well soon my dear friend!

John

P.S. I hope you are saving these letters
in a 3 ring binder!

Monday, Feb 22, 2010

Letter #4

Dear Bill,

Sometimes you're the dog...
Sometimes you're the hydrant.

When it comes to this cancer --
BE THE DOG!
Lick this thing!

— Praying for you! —

From your friend, John

← Don't forget! They are 3 hole punched ··· ready
to place in a binder!

Tuesday, Feb 23, 2010

Letter # 5

Dear Bill,

Life shrinks or expands
in proportion
to one's courage.

-Anaïs Nin-

TODAY, I pray for an
extra degree of courage
for you!

From your friend, John

Wednesday, Feb 24, 2010

Letter #6

Dear Bill,

IT'S NOT WHETHER YOU GET
KNOCKED DOWN,
IT'S WHETHER YOU GET UP AGAIN.

— VINCE LOMBARDI —

From your friend, John

Thursday, Feb 25 2010

Letter # 7

Dear Bill,

Some people
   complain that God put
                thorns on roses,
   while others praise Him
                for putting roses
                on thorns.

                        -Author Unknown-

From your friend, John

Friday, Feb 26, 2010

Letter #8

Dear Bill,
I thought you might like this cartoon:

Bill, I hope you find some way to laugh
at least an hour each day.

From your friend, John

Friday, Feb 27, 2010

Letter # 9

Dear Bill,

But they that wait upon the Lord
shall renew their strength;
they shall mount up with wings like eagles;
they shall run and not be weary;
and they shall walk and not faint.

-Isaiah 40:31 -

From your friend, John

Letter # 10

Dear Bill,

PRAYER

the ⚷ of the day
and the lock of the night.

—Thomas Fuller —

From your friend, John

Monday, Mar 1, 2010

Letter #11

Dear Bill,

GRATITUDE

Gratitude unlocks the fullness of life
It turns what we have into enough and more.
It turns denial into acceptance
chaos to order, confusion to clarity.
It can turn a meal into a feast,
a house into a home, a stranger into
a friend.   — MELODY BEATTIE —

Even during the toughest of times
in everything
cultivate an attitude
of

GRATITUDE

From your friend,   John

Letter # 12

Dear Bill,

LIFE
is'nt about
waiting for the storms
to pass,
It's about learning
how to dance
in the
rain.

From your friend, John

Letter # 13

Dear Bill,

"Jesus knows me, this I love!"

Enjoy
 the
  little
   things
    in
     life
     for
      someday
       you'll
        look
         back
          and
           realize
            they
             were
              the
              BIG
               things.

From your friend, John

Thursday, Mar 4, 2010

Letter # 14

Dear Bill,

When you wake up each morning

Check your pulse,

If you have a pulse,

You have a purpose!

— Paul Newman —

From your friend,   John

Friday, Mar 5, 2010

Letter # 15

Dear Bill,

NO GOD
NO PEACE
KNOW GOD
KNOW PEACE

-Author Unknown-

From your friend, John

Saturday, Mar 6, 2010

Letter # 16

Dear Bill,

We can only be said to be alive
     in those moments
          when our hearts are conscious
               of our treasures.

—THORNTON WILDER—

From your friend,   John

Sunday, Mar. 7, 2010

Letter # 17

Dear Bill,

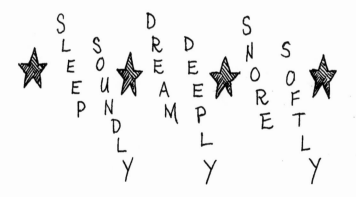

From your friend, John

Monday, Mar. 8, 2010

Letter #18

Dear Bill,

AGING...

FIRST - YOU FORGET NAMES,

THEN - YOU FORGET FACES,

THEN - YOU FORGET TO PULL YOUR ZIPPER UP ↑

THEN - YOU FORGET TO PULL YOUR ZIPPER DOWN ↓

From your friend, John

Tuesday, Mar 9, 2010

Letter #19

Dear Bill,

"Life is not measured
   by the number of breaths
   we take,

But by the moments
   that take
      our breath away."

— On Captain Kanya Reyes-emails —
   — U.S. Air Force —

From your friend, John

Wednesday, Mar. 10, 2010

Letter # 20

Dear Bill,

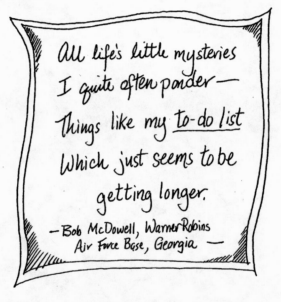

All life's little mysteries
I quite often ponder —
Things like my <u>to-do list</u>
Which just seems to be
getting longer.
— Bob McDowell, Warner Robins
Air Force Base, Georgia —

From your friend, John

P.S. Bill, I believe we both have
<u>TO DO LISTS</u> that will never run out!

Thursday, Mar 11, 2010

Letter # 21

Dear Bill,

When Peace,
        like a river,
attendeth my way.
When sorrows
        like sea billows roll;
whatever my lot,
Thou has taught me to say,
It is well,
    it is well
        with my soul.
                        —Horatio
                        G.
                        Spafford—

From your friend, John

Friday, Mar. 12, 2010

Letter # 22

Dear Bill,

No WINTER
  LASTS FOREVER;

No SPRING
    SKIPS ITS TURN.

—HAL BORLAND—

From your friend, John

Saturday, Mar. 13, 2010

Letter # 23

Dear Bill,

Life is short, Break the rules,
Forgive quickly, Kiss slowly,
Love truly, Laugh uncontrollably,
And never regret anything that
made you smile.
We never touch people so lightly that
we do not
leave a trace.

— AUTHOR UNKNOWN —

From your friend, John

Sunday, Mar. 14, 2010

Letter # 24

Dear Bill,

I AM NOT AFRAID OF STORMS
FOR I AM LEARNING HOW
TO SAIL MY SHIP.

—Louisa
May
Alcott—

From your friend, John

Monday, Mar 15, 2010

Letter #25

Dear Bill,

WHEN I DAILY
LIVE IN THE LIGHT
OF UNFOLDING MIRACLES,
THERE IS ALWAYS
A BRIGHT FUTURE,
ALWAYS A HOPE

- THOMAS KINKADE -
- PAINTER OF LIGHT -

From your friend, John

Tuesday, Mar 16, 2010

Letter #26

Dear Bill,

Small sign at restaurant
              check-out counter,
     next to cash register...

From your friend, John

Wednesday, Mar. 17, 2010

Letter #27

Dear Bill,

→ Something to think about...

EVERY SAINT HAS A PAST, AND
EVERY SINNER HAS A FUTURE.

— 16th Century Poet —

From your friend, John

Thursday, Mar 18, 2010

Letter # 28

Dear Bill,

To live
   is to arrive
      where everything
         begins;

To love
   is to go
      where nothing
         ever ends.

AUTHOR UNKNOWN

From your friend, John

Friday, Mar 19, 2010

Letter #29

Dear Bill,

Our **Longleaf** community
is a beautiful thing, sometimes
it even heals us and makes us
better
than we otherwise would be.

John Christian
(Just something I believe!)

From your friend, John

Saturday, Mar. 20, 2010

Letter # 30

Dear Bill,

LIFE IS ALL MEMORY
    except
    for the one present moment
    that goes by so quickly
    you hardly catch it going.

                    —Tennessee Williams—

From your friend, John

Sunday, Mar. 21, 2010

Letter #31

Dear Bill,

LIVE DEEP
INSTEAD OF FAST.

HENRY
SEIDEL
CANBY

From your friend, John

Monday, Mar. 22, 2010

Letter # 32

Dear Bill,

"You will seek Me
        and find Me
when you search for Me
        with all your heart"

— Jeremiah 29:13 —

From your friend, John

Tuesday, Mar. 23, 2010

Letter #33

Dear Bill,

Hitch Your Wagon

To A ⭐

— Ralph Waldo Emerson —

From your friend, John

Wednesday, Mar. 24, 2010

Letter # 34

Dear Bill,

Here is the test
to find
whether your mission on earth
is finished:
If you're alive,
it isn't.

— Richard Bach —

From your friend,   John

Thursday, Mar. 25, 2010

Letter #35

Dear Bill,

The supreme happiness of life
is the conviction
                    that we are loved.

— VICTOR ◊ HUGO —

From your friend, John

Friday, Mar 26, 2010

Letter #36

Dear Bill,

Death is more universal
                than life
Everyone dies
            but not everyone lives.

— Alan Sachs —

From your friend, John

Saturday, Mar. 27, 2010

Letter #37

Dear Bill,

Dreams

There are people
who put their dreams
in a little box and say,
"YES, I've got dreams,
of course I've got dreams!"
Then they put the little box away
and bring it out once in a while
to look in it,   and yep...

they're still there.

—ERMA
BOMBECK—

From your friend,   John

Sunday, Mar 28, 2010

Letter # 38

Dear Bill,

Never go to bed mad.
Stay up and fight!

~ phyllis diller ~

From your friend, John

Monday, Mar 29, 2010

Letter # 39

Dear Bill,

IF GOOD **Friends**
DON'T PURPOSELY GET TOGETHER
FROM TIME TO TIME,
THE DISTANCE STARTS TO GROW —
IT BECOMES A FEW WEEKS,
A MONTH, A YEAR — —
IT BECOMES
TOO
LATE!

— John Christian —
(Me, Myself)

From your friend, John

Tuesday, Mar. 30 2010

Letter # 40

Dear Bill,

Our Legacy
is determined
by how we spend
our Days.

From your friend, John

March 31, 2010

Letter # 41

Dear Bill,

Sometimes when life's worries
 Overshadow thought and heart,
 I search out a quiet place
 To get a fresh new start.

I open up His Holy Word
 And let His Peace flow in
 Then rested, ready, and renewed,
 I let the world back in.

— Janice Burns —

From your friend, John

Thursday, April 1, 2010

Letter # 42

Dear Bill,

When life
gives you LEMONS..
Smile politely,
then throw them away
When life isn't looking.

— Author Unknown —

From your friend, John

Friday, April 2, 2010

Letter #43

Dear Bill,

NOTHING

IS

WORTH

MORE

THAN

THIS

DAY!

— Johann Wolfgang Van Goethe —

From your friend, John

Saturday, April 3, 2010

Letter #44

Dear Bill,

When you come

to a 🍴 in the road,

take it.

— Yogi Berra —

Also from Yogi Berra:

IT'S LIKE DÉ JÁ VU ALL OVER AGAIN.

From your friend, John

Sunday, April 4, 2010

Letter # 45

Dear Bill,

I
child-proofed
my
home
and
they
still
get
in!

From your friend, John

Monday, April 5, 2010

Letter # 46

Dear Bill,

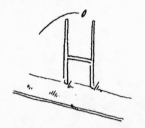

For when the One GREAT SCORER comes
to write against your name.
He marks — not that you won or lost
— but how you played the game.

— GRANTLAND RICE —

From your friend — John

Tuesday, April 6, 2010

Letter # 47

Dear Bill,

It's not whether
        you get knocked down,
It's whether
        you get up again.

                    Vince Lombardi

From your friend — John

Wednesday, April 7, 2010

Letter # 48

Dear Bill,

LOVE WHOLEHEARTEDLY,
BE SURPRISED,
GIVE THANKS
AND PRAISE.
THEN YOU WILL DISCOVER
THE FULNESS OF YOUR LIFE.

— BROTHER DAVID STEINDLE RAST —

From your friend, John

Thursday, April 8, 2010

Letter # 49

Dear Bill,

We should live
as those who are
on a journey home.
A home we know
will have the lights on
and the door open,
and our Father waiting for us
when we arrive.
That means in all our adversity
our worship of God is joyful,
our life hopeful, our future secure.
There is nothing we can lose on earth
that can rob us of the treasures
God has given and will give us.
    -AUTHOR UNKNOWN-   Amen!

From your friend, John

Friday, April 9, 2010

LETTER # 50

Dear Bill,

BE THE PERSON YOUR DOG THINKS YOU ARE!

From your friend, John

Friday, April 9, 2010

Dear Glenda,

Look towards the sun (son)
and the shadows
will always
fall behind you.

— Author Unknown —

From your friends, John & Peggy

Saturday, April 10, 2010

Letter # 51

Dear Bill,

We are too busy to pray,
And so we are too busy <u>to have power.</u>
We have a great deal of activity,
But we accomplish little;
Many services but few conversions;
Much machinery
        but few results

— R. A. Torrey —

From your friend, John

Sunday, April 11, 2010

Letter # 52

Dear Bill,

<u>Questions</u> and <u>Answers</u>

Q What is the secret of life?
  A Having good judgement.

Q How do you learn to have good judgement?
  A Through experience.

Q How do you obtain this experience?
  A Usually through bad judgement.

— Indian Parable —

From your friend, John

Monday, April 12, 2010

Letter # 53

Dear Bill,

◙ ATTITUDE ◙

Two stonecutters were asked what they were doing.

The first said: "I'm cutting this stone into blocks."

The second replied: "I'm building a cathedral."

- OLD STORY -

From your friend, John

Tuesday, April 13, 2010

Letter # 54

Dear Bill,

HOW COME?

EVERY TIME I PRAY
MY HORIZON IS ALTERED,
MY ATTITUDE IS ALTERED,
NOT SOMETIMES,
BUT EVERYTIME!
AND THE AMAZING / PUZZLING THING
IS THAT I DON'T PRAY MORE.

From your friend, John

Wednesday, April 14, 2010

Letter # 55

Dear Bill,

In the quiet of this day
may you know the greatness
of your spirit,
and may your hopes
fly on the wings
of
possibility.

Mary
Anne
Radmacher

From your friend, John

Thursday, April 15, 2010

Letter #56

Dear Bill,

WOMEN DEPRIVED OF THE COMPANY OF MEN, PINE.

MEN DEPRIVED OF THE COMPANY OF WOMEN, BECOME STUPID.

ANTON CHEKHOV —

From your friend, John

Friday, April 16, 2010

Letter # 57

Dear Bill,

ON LOVE...

Don't look at love as a trickling stream
...but when love comes
   may it be gushing — huge,
a flood, a torrent, overflowing
its banks, uncontained and relentless —
overwhelming, unbridled, never-ending,
                    eternal.
   This is love — at its very best!
            — by John Christian —

From your friend, John

Saturday, April 17, 2010

Letter # 58

Dear Bill,

MARRIAGE

MARRIAGE
IS
AN
EMPTY
BOX.

IT
REMAINS
EMPTY
UNLESS
YOU
PUT
IN
MORE
THAN
YOU
TAKE
OUT.

From
Your Friend,
John

H. JACKSON BROWN

Sunday, April 18, 2010

Letter # 59

Dear Bill,

A man scheduled a plumber
to do some work at his home.
The plumber did a little over an hours
worth of work, fixed the problem,
then handed the man the bill. The man
stared in disbelief at the bill which was
over #300.00 and complained. "Why, I'm
a DOCTOR, and I've never made that
Kind of money!" The plumber replied,
"When I was a doctor I never made
that Kind of money either!"

From your friend, John

Monday, April 19, 2010

Letter # 60

Dear Bill,

Achieving Success

He has achieved success
who has
lived well,
laughed often
and
loved much

— BESSIE ANDERSON STANLEY —

From your friend, John

Tuesday, April 20, 2010

Letter #61

Dear Bill,

We make a living
by what we get,
But we make a life
by what we give.

From your friend, John

P.S. What a great golf cart. I know
you are enjoying it!

Wednesday, April 21, 2010

Letter # 62

Dear Bill,

Here is one of my favorite scriptures. Peggy and I pray for You and Glenda each morning. I know that complete and total healing for you is possible and may have even taken place by now. I know that God is sustaining and comforting you!

— PSALM 5:3 —

IN THE MORNING, O LORD, YOU HEAR MY VOICE;
IN THE MORNING I LAY MY REQUESTS BEFORE YOU
AND WAIT IN EXPECTATION.

Amen!

There is something extra special about praying in the quiet and still of morning
...and make sure to listen!

From your friend, John

Thursday, April 22, 2010

Letter #63

Dear Bill,

Something to think about:

IF GOD IS NOT IN CONTROL, <u>THEN WHO IS</u>?

From your friend, John

Friday, April 23, 2010

Letter # 64

Dear Bill,

I am today where my thoughts
                have brought me;

I will be tomorrow where my thoughts
                take me.

— AUTHOR UNKNOWN —

From your friend, John

Saturday, April 24, 2010

Letter # 65

Dear Bill,

"By
   all
      means
         marry;
            if you
            get a
               good wife,
                  you'll be
                     happy;
                  if you
            get
         a
         bad one,
      you can
   become
a
philosopher!"

— SOCRATES —

From your friend, John

Sunday, April 25, 2010

Letter # 66

Dear Bill,

A HERO IS NO BRAVER
        THAN ORDINARY MEN,
        BUT HE IS BRAVE
        FIVE MINUTES LONGER.

        RALPH
        WALDO
        EMERSON

From your friend, John

Letter # 67

Dear Bill,

IF THERE
    ARE NO DOGS
IN HEAVEN,
    THEN
WHEN I DIE
    I WANT
TO GO
    WHERE
        THEY WENT.

WILL
ROGERS

From your friend, John

Tuesday, April 27, 2010

Letter # 68

Dear Bill,

I WONDER
IF GOD
LEANED OVER
TO GABRIEL
AFTER
CREATING EVE
AND SAID, "OOPS!"

From your friend, John

Wednesday, April 28 2010

Letter # 69

Dear Bill,

The true measure
        of success in life
        is not what you have,
but what you can do without.

— AUTHOR UNKNOWN —

From your friend, John

Thursday, April 29, 2010

Letter #70

Dear Bill,

OUR PERFECT COMPANIONS
NEVER HAVE
FEWER THAN FOUR FEET.

— COLETTE —

From your friend, John

Friday, Apr. 30 2010

Letter # 71

Dear Bill,

" If you think
EDUCATION
is expensive,
wait 'til you see
what
IGNORANCE
costs you."

— John M. Capozzi —

From your friend, John

Saturday, May 1, 2010

Letter # 72

Dear Bill,

IF
 YOU
   DON'T
    CHEW
      YOUR
       FOOD
         WELL,
        WHO
          WILL?

— AUTHOR ? —

From your friend, John

Sunday, May 2, 2010

LETTER # 73

Dear Bill,

A SMILE IS THE LIGHT

IN THE WINDOW

OF YOUR FACE

THAT TELLS PEOPLE

THAT YOUR HEART

IS AT HOME.

- AUTHOR UNKNOWN

From your friend, John

Monday, May 3, 2010

LETTER # 74

Dear Bill,

PRAYER

LORD, DELIVER ME FROM THE MAN
WHO NEVER MAKES A MISTAKE
AND ALSO FROM THE MAN WHO
MAKES THE SAME MISTAKE
                    TWICE.

- WILLIAM MAYO -

From your friend, John

Tuesday, May 4, 2010

Letter # 75

Dear Bill,

PRAYER IS NOT A <u>MONOLOGUE</u>
BUT A <u>DIALOGUE</u>; GOD'S VOICE
IN RESPONSE TO MINE
IS ITS MOST ESSENTIAL PART.
LISTENING TO GOD'S VOICE
IS THE SECRET OF THE
ASSURANCE THAT HE
WILL LISTEN
TO MINE.

— ANDREW MURRAY —

From your friend,   John

Wednesday, May 5, 2010

Letter # 76

Dear Bill,

HORSE SENSE

HORSE SENSE
        IS WHAT A HORSE HAS

THAT KEEPS HIM
        FROM BETTING
                ON PEOPLE.

                — W. C. FIELDS —

From your friend, John

Thursday, May 6, 2010

Letter # 77

Dear Bill,

ONE CAN GO A LONG WAY

AFTER ONE IS TIRED

- FRENCH PROVERB -

From your friend, John

Friday, May 7, 2010

Letter # 78

Dear Bill,

THE OPTIMIST PROCLAIMS
THAT WE LIVE IN THE BEST
OF ALL POSSIBLE WORLDS;
AND THE DESSIMIST
FEARS THIS IS TRUE.

James
Branch
Cabell

From your friend, John

Saturday, May 8, 2012

Letter # 79

Dear Bill,

We do not remember Days,
We remember Moments

-Cesare Pavese-

From your friend, John

Sunday, May 9, 2012

Letter # 80

Dear Bill,

An unrepentent scoffer
announced that God is no where.
But one saved and
washed in the blood
of the Lamb
announced that God is now here.

– Author Unknown –

From your friend, John

Monday, May 10, 2010

Letter # 81

Dear Bill,

Sometimes I wake up
GROUCHY,
Sometimes I let her
sleep - in.

-Author unknown-

From your friend, John

Tuesday, May 11, 2010

Letter # 82

Dear Bill,

A single rose
    can be my garden ...
A single friend,
    my world.

                    Leo
                    Buscaglia

From your friend, John

Wednesday, May 12, 2010

Letter # 83

Dear Bill,

Some people
make things happen.
Some just watch
while things happen,
and Some wonder at the
end of life.....

WHAT HAPPENNED?

BILL, YOU & GLENDA MAKE THINGS HAPPEN!
THATS WHAT I LIKE ABOUT YOU BOTH!

From your friend, John

Thursday, May 13, 2010

Letter # 84

Dear Bill,

My dog
is worried about
the economy
and the high cost of living.
"Alpo" now costs $3.00 per can
Thats $21.00
in dog money.

(AUTHOR)
(UNKNOWN)

From your friend, John

Friday, May 14, 2010

Letter # 85

Dear Bill,

FRIENDSHIP IS
A COZY SHELTER
FROM
LIFE'S RAINY DAYS.

From your friend, John

Saturday, May 15, 2010

Letter # 86

Dear Bill,

I MUST

spread out my petition
before God
and then say:

"THY WILL, NOT MINE, BE DONE!"

I MUST

learn
to let
the Lord
choose for me.   by John Christian

From your friend, John

Sunday, May 16, 2010

Letter # 87

Dear Bill,

Yesterday is history.
Tomorrow is a mystery.
Today is a gift.
That's why we call it
"The Present"

AUTHOR
UNKNOWN

From your friend, John

Monday, May 17, 2010

Letter # 88

Dear Bill,

LORD help me live from day to day
in such a self-forgetful way,
that even when I kneel to pray,
my prayer shall be for others.

CHARLES
DELUCENA
MEIGS

From your friend, John

Tuesday, May 18, 2010

Letter #89

Dear Bill,

ADVERSITY

CAUSES SOME MEN TO BREAK,
OTHERS TO BREAK RECORDS.

From your friend, John

Wednesday, May 19, 2010

Letter # 90

Dear Bill,

It's
not
the
load
that
breaks
you
down,
it's
the
way
you
carry
it.   Lena Horne

From your friend, John

Thursday, May 20, 2010
Letter # 91

Dear Bill,

THERE'S A LIGHT BEHIND EVERY SHADOW.

From your friend, John

Friday, May 21, 2010

Letter # 92

Dear Bill,

When I
see my
LIFE
as a
series of
unfolding
MIRACLES
I'll always
sail forth
with hope,
tranquility,
THOMAS   and joy
KINKADE   in my
♡ heart

From your friend, John

Saturday, May 22, 2010

Letter # 93

Dear Bill,

3 _real_ children's letters to God:

(1) Dear God,   Instead of letting people die
and having to make new ones, why
don't you just keep the ones you got now?
— Jane —

(2) Dear God, I think the stapler is one of
your greatest inventions.
— Ruth M. —

(3) Dear God, Thank you for the baby
brother, but what I prayed for was
a puppy. — Joyce —

From your friend, John

Sunday, May 23, 2010

Letter # 94

Dear Bill,

When
a
piece of Heaven
falls to
earth it
becomes
a Garden
—Anon—

just like our
very own
Callaway Gardens!

From your friend, John

Monday, May 24, 2012

Letter # 95

Dear Bill,

He that has light
    within his own clear breast
        may sit i' th' centre
and enjoy
a bright day.

— JOHN MILTON —

From your friend, John

Tuesday, May 25, 2010

Letter # 96

Dear Bill,

3 more _real_ children's letters to God:

(1) Dear God, I bet it is very hard for you to love all of the people in the whole world. There are only 4 people in our family and I can never do it.
—Nan—

(2) Dear God, If you watch in church Sunday, I will show you my new shoes.
—Sally D.—

(3) Dear God, If we come back as something — please don't let it be Jennifer Horton because I hate her.
— Denise —

From your friend, John

Wednesday, May 26, 2010

Letter # 97

Dear Bill,

"All shall be well,
and all shall be well,
and all manner of things
shall be well."

Julian of Norwich
- 14th Century -

From your friend, John

Thursday, May 27, 2010

Letter # 98

Dear Bill,

PRAYER

Lord, draw me into the
inner-most chambers of your
heart, and
fill me afresh Today
with your Holy Spirit.

Amen!

From your friend, John

Friday, May 28, 2010

Letter # 99

Dear Bill,

No
  Matter
    Where
      I
        Take
          My
            Guests.....It
                    Seems
                      They
                        Like
                          My
                            Kitchen
                              Best!

From your friend, John

Saturday, May 29, 2010

Letter #100

Dear Bill,

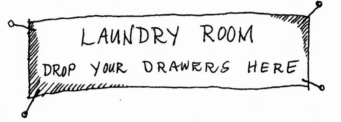

From your friend, John

Saturday, May 29, 2010

Letter # 100

Dear Glenda,
        This morning I say a special prayer
for you ... but I also make you __this__
        __promise:__

        Eat a live Frog each morning
                and

nothing worse will happen to you
                the rest
                of the day.

* I'VE NEVER TRIED IT - BUT I THINK IT WILL WORK.

From your friend, John

Sunday, May 30, 2010

Letter # 101

Dear Bill,

Here's to the tall ships
Here's to the small ships
Here's to all the ships at sea.
But the best ships
are friendships...
Here's to you and me.

MARITIME ⚓ BLESSING

Bill you are truly a dear friend!

From your friend,   John

Tuesday, June 2, 2010

Letter # 103

Dear Bill,

A Thought To Remember

No husband
   has ever been shot
      While doing
         The dishes.

From your friend, John

P.S. Peggy and I continue to pray for you and Glenda
daily --- Complete, miraculous healing and peace for
you --- courage, strength, and peace for Glenda.

Wednesday, Jun 3, 2010

Letter # 104

Dear Bill,

    I strongly believe
      WE HONOR GOD more, when
we ask for great things (like a miraculous
cure for cancer) rather than just asking
for the little things --- though both
are important and prayer worthy. We
must remember that He created 100 billion
or more galaxies with over 100 billion stars
in each --- He is also the Great
Physician and Our Father, Who really
wants the best for each of us.
                    Amen!

From your friend, John

Thursday, June 3, 2010

Letter # 105

Dear Bill,

NO MATTER
HOW TALL THE
MOUNTAIN,
IT CANNOT BLOCK OUT THE SUN (SON).

From your friend, John

Friday June 4, 2010
Letter #105

Dear Bill,

When you can't
change the direction
of the wind —
ADJUST YOUR SAILS.

From your friend, John

Saturday, Jan 5, 2010

Letter # 106

Dear Bill,

There are only 2 things
in the world
to worry over:
1) The things you can control, and

2) The things you can't control.

Fix the 1st,

Forget the 2nd!

AUTHOR UNKNOWN

From your friend, John

Sunday, June 6, 2010
Letter # 107

Dear Bill,

You will do -CREATIVITY-
foolish things
but do them
with enthusiasm!

- COLETTE -

From your friend, John

Monday, June 7, 2010

Letter # 108

Dear Bill,

LOVE DOES NOT
CONSIST IN
GAZING AT
EACH OTHER,
BUT
IN LOOKING
TOGETHER
IN THE
          SAME
              DIRECTION.

— ANTOINE DE ST. EXUPERY —

From your friend, John

Tuesday, June 8, 2010

Letter # 109

Dear Bill,

BUT WHAT IS HAPPINESS?
EXCEPT THE SIMPLE HARMONY
BETWEEN A MAN
AND THE LIFE
HE LEADS

— ALBERT CAMUS —

From your friend, John

Wednesday, June 9, 2010

Letter # 110

Dear Bill,

Remember always that you have not
only the right to be an
individual; you have an
obligation to be one
You cannot make any
useful contribution in
life unless you do this.

~ ELEANORE ROOSEVELT ~

From your friend, John

Thursday, June 10, 2010

Letter # 111

Dear Bill,

A baby
is God's opinion
that the world
should go on.
—Carl Sandburg—

From your friend, John

Friday, June 11, 2010
Letter #112

Dear Bill,

As I grow older,
and reflect on my life
and my Christian faith,
it has settled in my spirit,
and I believe it to be
a Great Truth
that to really fulfill
my purpose here and
to have great peace and joy,
my life MUST be a life of service ---
and this is especially true
of my retirement years.
                        — John Christian —

From your friend, John

Saturday, June 12, 2010

Letter # 113

Dear Bill

It is
a very funny
thing about life:
If you
refuse to accept
anything but the best
you very often
get it.

— W.
SOMERSET
MAUGHAM

From your friend, John

Sunday, June 13, 2010

Letter # 115

Dear Bill,

The Inner Life

Inside myself
is a place where I live all alone
and renew the springs
that <u>never</u> dry up.

PEARL
S.
BUCK

From your friend, John

Monday, June 14, 2010
Letter # 116

Dear Bill,

To play great music,
You must keep your eyes
On a distant star

Yehudi Menuhin

From your friend, John

Tuesday, June 15 2010

Letter #117

Dear Bill,

Here is a poem written by the daughter of a good friend of mine --- back in the early 70's. I thought it was quite special and have kept it all of these years.

WHO KNOWS THE WIND?
DOES IT BLOW MUSIC?
DOES IT BLOW WIND?
IT BLOWS MUSIC.
   I CAN HEAR IT.

                    - BARBARA - AGE 4 YRS & 10 MONTHS -

From your friend, John

Wednesday, June 16, 2010

Letter # 118

Dear Bill,

I believe this is the world's
shortest poem:

ADAM
HAD 'EM.
— by Strickland W. Gilliland —

I hope that You and Glenda have a
wonderful and blessed day!

From your friend, John

Thursday, June 17, 2010

Letter # 119

Dear Bill,

There are ✫ stars
whose radiance is visible on earth
though they have been long extinct.

There are people whose brilliance
continues to light the world
though they are no longer
among the living.

These lights are particularly bright
when the night is dark.

— HANNAH SENESCH ✫

From your friend, John

Friday, June 18, 2010

Letter #120

Dear Bill,

How long is a Minute?

How long a minute is
    Depends on which side
        Of the bathroom door
            You're on.

OCCUPIED

From your friend, John

Saturday, June 19, 2010

Letter # 121

Dear Bill,

If all
the world's
a
stage,

I want
to operate
the trap door.

— AUTHOR UNKNOWN —

From your friend, John

Sunday, June 20, 2010

Letter # 121

Dear Bill,

"The WORD OF GOD is
   simple, straight forward and clear--
so clear that a babe in Christ
   can wade in the water --
yet deep enough for theologians
   to swim in forever
and never touch bottom.

(From my Sermon Notes--- spoken by Rural Ansley, Pastor,
First United Methodist Church, Sunday Worship, Feb 26, 2006)
Niceville, Florida

From your friend, John

Monday, June 21, 2010

Letter # 122

Dear Bill,

You grow up
the day you have
your first real laugh
at
yourself

— ETHEL BARRYMORE —

From your friend, John

Tuesday, June 22, 2010

Letter # 123

Dear Bill,

You can tell the ideals of a nation
by its advertisements.

— NORMAN DOUGLAS —

From your friend, John

Wednesday, June 23, 2010

Letter # 124

Dear Bill,

I am so absorbed
    in the wonder of earth
        and the life upon it
          that I cannot think of heaven
    and the angels.
I have enough for this life.

$$\begin{pmatrix} PEARL \\ S. \\ BUCK \end{pmatrix}$$

From your friend, John

Thursday, June 24, 2010

Letter # 125

Dear Bill,

IT HAS ALWAYS
SEEMED TO ME
THAT THE MOST
DIFFICULT PART
OF BUILDING
A BRIDGE
WOULD BE
THE START.

— ROBERT BENCHLEY —

From your friend, John

Friday, June 25, 2010

Letter # 126

Dear Bill,

Something to Think About...

Experience
is
what
you
got
by
not
having
it
when
you
needed
it.
                    —Author-Unknown—

From your friend, John

Saturday, June 26, 2010

Letter #127

Dear Bill,

The
HAPPINESS
of my life
depends on the
QUALITY
of my thoughts!

-AUTHOR UNKNOWN-

From your friend, John

Sunday, June 27, 2010

Letter #128

Dear Bill,

There are <u>2 ways</u> to be rich:
make more or
desire less.

— AUTHOR UNKNOWN —

From your friend, John

Monday, June 28, 2010

Letter # 130

Dear Bill,

TIME you _enjoyed_ wasting

was _not_ wasted.

~— John Lennon —~

From your friend, John

P.S. I prayed for you this morning... _Again_:
Be healed my friend --- Be whole
and complete --- in Jesus name! _Amen!_

Tuesday, June 29, 2010

Letter # 131

Dear Bill,

"I think it pisses God off

if you walk

by the color purple

in a field somewhere

and don't notice

it."

⟶ ALICE WALKER, AUTHOR: "THE COLOR PURPLE" ⟵

From your friend, John

Wednesday, June 30, 2010

Letter # 132

Dear Bill,

Everyone must carry two pieces of
   paper with him and
   look at them every day.
   On one it is written:
      "You are as dust and ashes."
               and on the other:
   "For you the world was created."
                        ← Rabbinic
                         Saying →

From your friend, John

Thursday, July 1, 2010

Letter # 133

Dear Bill,

Peggy saw a bumper sticker Tuesday morning. I wrote it in my Journal _and_ thought you might enjoy it too:

WAG MORE,

BARK LESS

From your friend, John

Thursday, July 1, 2010

Letter # 133

Dear Bill,

My prayer for you today is not only that you will be healed and whole again, but that you will also continue to have great courage.

COURAGE is being scared to death and saddling up anyway.

— JOHN WAYNE —

From your friend, John

Friday, July 2, 2010

Letter # 134

Dear Bill,

"If a man does not keep pace
with his companions,
Perhaps it is because he hears
a different drummer.
Let him step to the music
which he hears,
however measured
or far away."

— HENRY DAVID THOREAU —

From your friend — John

Saturday, July 3, 2010

Letter # 135

Dear Bill,

Hand over the chocolate,

and no one will get hurt!

also

Eat, drink, and be merry...

for tomorrow

we diet.

From your friend, John

Sunday, July 4, 2010

Letter # 136

Dear Bill and Glenda,

Happy 4th of July!
Isn't it wonderful to live in
a free country?

And while you are celebrating with
family and friends, please
keep in mind that:

BROKEN COOKIES HAVE NO CALORIES.

From your friend, John

Monday, July 5, 2010

Letter # 137

Dear Bill,

We make a living
      by what we get.
We make a life
      by what we give.

From your friend, John

Tuesday, July 6, 2010

Letter # 138

Dear Bill,

　You may not want to share this with Glenda ---
but, then again you may...

　　The 3 Rings of Marriage :

　　　◎ The Engagement Ring

　　　◎ The Wedding Ring　(Author Unknown)

　　　◎ The Suffe Ring

　　　　　　　　　　Ha!

-Although you and I both know Glenda
　　　has been really good for you !

From your friend, John

Wednesday, July 7, 2010

Letter # 139

Dear Bill,

 IS WHERE A GUY
GETS STABBED IN THE BACK
AND INSTEAD OF DYING,
HE SINGS.

- Robert Benchley -

From your friend, John

Get well soon,
if you're not
already!

Thursday, July 8, 2010

Letter # 140

Dear Bill,

My wife

says I never

listen to her.

At least I think thats what she said.

– AUTHOR UNKNOWN –

From your friend, John

Friday, July 9, 2010

Letter # 141

Dear Bill,

God grant me
    the serenity to
        accept the people
    I cannot change,
        the courage to change
    the one I can,
and the **WISDOM**
    to know it's me ___.

- AUTHOR UNKNOW - A VARIATION ON THE "SERENITY PRAYER" -
- BY REINHOLD NEIBUR -

From your friend, John

Saturday, July 10, 2010

Letter # 142

Dear Bill,

Here are _perhaps_
the **7** most powerful
words in the world:

TAKE 100% RESPONSIBILITY FOR YOUR ENTIRE LIFE.
— Jack Canfield —

Our _nation_ and _world_ would be a whole lot better if
we would _all_ do this!

From your friend, John

Sunday, July 11, 2010

Letter # 143

Dear Bill,

   He who sacrifices
      his conscience to ambition
   Burns a picture
            to obtain the ashes.

            —— Chinese Proverb ——

From your friend, John

Monday, July 12, 2010

Letter #144

Dear Bill,

The Lord is my Shepherd.....

—from the beginning line of the 23rd Psalm.—

Even the shortest, simplest phrase from the
Bible speaks volumes!

From your friend, John

Tuesday, July 13, 2010

Letter # 145

Dear Bill,

Here is another one:

In the beginning God.....

(from Genesis 1:1)

IT SORT OF SAYS IT ALL!

From your friend, John

Wednesday, July 14, 2010

Letter # 146

Dear Bill,

REVELATION 22:13

I AM ALPHA AND OMEGA,
THE BEGINNING AND THE END,
THE FIRST AND THE LAST.

Amen!

From your friend, John

Thursday, July 15, 2010

Letter # 147

Dear Bill,

HISTORY REPEATS ITSELF

AND THAT'S ONE OF THE THINGS

THAT'S WRONG

WITH HISTORY.

Clarence
Darrow

From your friend, John

Friday, July 16, 2010

Letter #148

Dear Bill,

Be not afraid of growing slowly,

Be afraid only

of standing still.

– CHINESE PROVERB –

From your friend, John

Saturday, July 17, 2010

Letter # 149

Dear Bill,

THINK. IT GIVES
YOU SOMETHING
TO DO
WHEN
YOUR COMPUTER
HAS "CRASHED!"

AUTHOR
UNKNOWN

From your friend, John

Sunday, July 18, 2010

Letter # 150

Dear Bill,

We block
our Dream
when we allow
our fears
to grow bigger
than our Faith.

—Adapted from a quote by Mary Manin Morrissey—

From your friend, John

Monday, July 19, 2010

Letter # 151

Dear Bill,

Praise the Lord,
O my Soul,
and forget not all His benefits —
who forgives all your sins
and Heals all your diseases.

PSALM 103: 2-3

Bill — We continue to pray for miraculous healing for you!

From your friend, John

Tuesday, July 20, 2010

Letter #152

Dear Bill,

IRISH TOAST

Health to you and yours;
to mine and ours.
If mine and ours ever comes across
you and yours,
I hope that you and yours
will do as much
for mine and ours,
As mine and ours have done
for you and yours. (Author unknown)

—For our dear friends, Bill and Glenda—

From your friend, John

Wednesday, July 21, 2010
Letter # 153

Dear Bill,

The sweetest sounds
to mortals given
are heard in

MOTHER,
HOME, and
HEAVEN.

—William Goldsmith Brown—

From your friend, John

Thursday, July 22, 2010

Letter # 154

Dear Bill,

Here is another quote about <u>ashes</u> from
a different author:

ANYTHING

> you do not give freely
> and abundantly
> becomes lost to you,
> You open your safe
> and find ashes. ⟨Anne Dillard⟩

From your friend, John

Friday, July 23, 2010

Letter #155

Dear Bill,

The idea that many people have that life is a vale of tears is just as false as the idea which the great majority have, and to which youth, health, and wealth incline you, that <u>life is a place of entertainment.</u> Life is a place of SERVICE, where one sometimes has occasion to put up with a lot that is hard, but more often to experience a great many JOYS. (Leo Tolstoy in a letter to his son, 1887)

From your friend, John

Saturday, July 24, 2010

Letter # 156

Dear Bill,

DIFFICULTY TIMES

Difficult times
    have helped me to understand
        better than before
how infinitely rich and beautiful life is
    in every way and that so many things
        that one goes worrying about
are of <u>no importance</u>
    whatsoever.

— Isak
    Dinesen —

From your friend, John

Sunday, July 25, 2010

Letter # 157

Dear Bill,

To
the
world
you may be
just one person,
but to one person
you may be
the
world.

— AUTHOR UNKNOWN —

From your friend,   John

Monday, July 26, 2010

Letter # 158

Dear Bill,

Live
in such a way
that those who know you
but don't know God,
will come to know God,
Because they know you......
And that way is *Love*!

- Author Unknown -

From your friend, John

Tuesday, July 29, 2010

Letter # 159

Dear Bill,

DINNER IS READY
WHEN
THE SMOKE ALARM
GOES OFF.

-AUTHOR UNKNOWN-

From your friend, John

Wednesday, July 28, 2010

Letter # 160

Dear Bill,

I don't repeat gossip,
        so listen carefully.

                    - Author Unknown -

From your friend, John

Thursday, July 29, 2010

Letter # 161

Dear Bill,

When angry
count to four.
When very angry
swear!

— MARK TWAIN —

From your friend, John

Friday July 30, 2010

Letter # 162

Dear Bill,

THE PROBLEM WITH PEOPLE WHO
HAVE <u>NO</u> VICES IS THAT GENERALLY
YOU CAN BE SURE
THEY'RE GOING TO HAVE SOME

PRETTY ANNOYING VIRTUES.

~ Elizabeth Taylor ~

From your friend, John

Saturday, July 31, 2010

Letter # 163

Dear Bill,

This isn't clutter ---
These are my priceless
antiques.

— AUTHOR UNKNOWN —

From your friend, John

Sunday, August 1, 2010

Letter # 164

Dear Bill,

All things bright and beautiful

All creatures great and small,

All things wise and wonderful,

the Lord God

made them all.

From your friend, John

Monday, August 2, 2010

Letter # 165

Dear Bill

THE WORLD IS A BOOK   READ BUT ONE PAGE.

THOSE WHO DO NOT TRAVEL

- St. Augustine -

From your friend, John

Tuesday, August 3, 2010

Letter # 166

Dear Bill,

A balanced diet
is a
cookie in each
hand.

From your friend, John

Wednesday, August 4, 2010

Letter # 167

Dear Bill,

Definition of Success

He has achieved success who has lived well, laughed often, and loved much; who has enjoyed the trust of pure women, the respect of intelligent men, and the love of little children; who has filled his niche and accomplished his task; who has left the world better than he found it, whether an improved poppy, a perfect person, or a rescued soul; who has always looked for the best in others and given them the best he had; whose life was an inspiration; whose memory a benediction.

— BESSIE ANDERSON STANLEY —

From your friend, John

Saturday, August 7, 2010

Dear Bill,

THERE IS ALWAYS
ALWAYS
ALWAYS
SOMETHING
TO BE THANKFUL FOR

From your friend, John

Thursday, August 5, 2010

Letter # 168

Good morning Bill,

Today many are praying for you. Our prayer is for <u>miraculous healing of brain cancer</u>, for courage, peace, and wholeness!

<u>Remember</u>, breathe in healing
breathe out illness

"<u>Dear Lord</u>,
take care of me,
the sea is so wide,
and my boat is so small."
Amen!

From your friend, John

Friday, August 6, 2010

Letter # 169

Dear Bill,

I'd Rather...
I'd rather see a sermon
than hear one;
I'd rather someone walk with me
than tell me the way.

— EDGAR A GUEST —

From your friend, John

Sunday, August 8, 2010

Letter # 171

Dear Bill,

When
things
are
too
good,
faith and spiritual concerns
suffer...
unless there is thunder, people
don't make
the sign of the cross.

— Catholic Priest —

From your friend, John

Sunday, August 8, 2010

Letter # 171

Dear Bill,

If you're going to try
cross-country
skiing —
start
with a
small country.

— Anonymous —

From your friend,   John

Monday, August 9, 2010

Letter # 172

Dear Bill,

IT IS
   ONE OF
      THE BLESSINGS
         OF OLD FRIENDS
            THAT YOU
               CAN AFFORD
            TO BE
         STUPID
      WITH THEM.

                        -Ralph
                          Waldo
                            Emerson -

From your friend, John

Tuesday, August 10, 2010

Letter #173

Dear Bill,

ONE MORNING
IN SUNDAY SCHOOL
WALTER SAID:

"Getting old will improve your prayer life."

— Walter Cleveland —

From your friend, John

Wednesday, August 11, 2010

Letter # 174

Dear Bill,

WHEN YOU "STUMBLE" MAKE IT PART OF THE DANCE.

— Author Unknown —

From your friend, John

Thursday, August 12, 2010

Letter #175

Dear Bill,

Husband & Wife
Together for Life.

-Anonymous-

From your friend, John

Friday, August 13, 2010

Letter #176

Dear Bill,

> GOD DOESN'T GIVE US
> WHAT WE CAN HANDLE;
> GOD HELPS US HANDLE
> WHAT WE ARE GIVEN.
>
> ANONYMOUS

From your friend, John

Saturday, August 14, 2010

Letter # 177

Dear Bill,

The TRUTH is finally out:
The _lower_ one's pants
    The _lower_ one's IQ!

Duh!

From your friend, John

Sunday, August 15, 2010

Letter #178

Dear Bill,

NEVER BE AFRAID
TO TRUST AN UNKOWN FUTURE
TO A KNOWN GOD.

— CORRIE
TEN
BOOM —

From your friend, John

Monday, August 16, 2010

Letter # 179

Dear Bill,

When running in the race of life,
    And faced with all it's toil and strife,
It may seem that the thing to do,
    Is give up running half-way through.
But that is when you need to pray
    And ask the Lord for strength <u>this day</u>,
To run the race until it's done
    And claim the victory you have won.
— Edward
    Ellis —

      Bill and Glenda, I'm proud of you
both -- you have responded with
courage, enthusiasm, and faith during this
<u>tough</u> time in your life. You <u>complete</u>
        healing and wholeness

From your friend, John ——— is on its way !

Tuesday, August 17, 2010

Letter #180

Dear Bill,

In prayer
it is better to
have a heart
without words
than words
without heart. —John Bunyan—

From your friend, John

Wednesday, August 18, 2010

Letter #180

Dear Bill,

I wonder
if God made Adam first
so He didn't have to listen
to Eve
telling Him how to do it?

From your friend, John

Thursday, August 19, 2010

Letter # 182

Dear Bill,

LIVE SIMPLY

LOVE GENEROUSLY

CARE DEEPLY

SPEAK KINDLY

LEAVE THE REST

TO **GOD**!

From your friend, John

Friday, August 20, 2010

Letter #183

Dear Bill,

Be still and know that I AM God.
Be still and know that I AM.
Be still and know.
Be still.
Be.

Psalm: 46:10

Meditate on This! ↗

From your friend John

Saturday, August 21, 2010

Letter # 184

Dear Bill,

I am only one,
but still I am one.
I cannot do everything,
but still I can do something;

I WILL NOT
REFUSE
TO DO
THE SOMETHING
I CAN DO.

—Helen Keller—

From your friend, John

Sunday, August 22, 2010

Letter # 185

Dear Bill,

All his earthly past
       will have been Heaven
to those who are saved...
       the good man's path begins to change
so that his forgiven sins
       and remembered sorrows
take on the quality of Heaven...
       at the end of all things,
the blessed will say,
"We never lived anywhere but in Heaven."

— C.S. Lewis —

From your friend, John

Monday, August 23, 2010

Letter # 186

Dear Bill,

As Christians —
Our Lives
Are The Books
People Read
Every Day.

From your friend, John

Tuesday, August 24, 2010

Letter # 187

Dear Bill,

As a rule
   Man's a fool
      When it's hot
         He wants it cool,
            When it's cool,
               He wants it hot
Always wanting...
What is not!   —Author Unknown—

IT WON'T BE LONG NOW... 85° HIGH FOR THE DAY,
            62° LOW FOR THE NIGHT ! CAN'T WAIT !

From your friend, John

Dear Bill,

The worst thing
that could possibly
happen to you,
could be the best thing
for you,
if
you don't let it
get the best
　　　　of you.

　　　　　　　—AUTHOR
　　　　　　　UNKNOWN—

From your friend, John

Thursday, August 26, 2010

Letter # 189

Dear Bill,

TODAY IS YESTERDAY'S

—THINK ABOUT IT — TOMORROW.

From your friend, John

Friday, August 27, 2010

Letter # 190

Dear Bill,
   I have been praying for <u>miraculous healing</u> for you for 190 days now, some days more than once. <u>Others</u> have been too! One of them is bound to take... so we'll Keep praying!

ISAIAH 40:31
   My <u>hope</u> is in the Lord,
     He will renew my strength.
I will soar on wings like eagles.
I will run and not grow weary.
I will walk and not faint.
     -PRAISE THE LORD-
        <u>Amen!</u>

From your friend, John

Saturday, August 28, 2010

Letter # 191

Dear Bill,

 "The strings of life
can be compared to the
strings of a violin.
They need to be tuned
time and time again."

— AUTHOR
UNKNOWN —

From your friend, John

Sunday, August 29, 2010

Letter # 192

Dear Bill,

Dilemna
by
David Budbill

I want to be
        famous
so I can be
        humble
about being
        famous. . .
What good is my humility
        when I am stuck
            in this obscurity?

From your friend, John

Monday, August 30, 2010

Letter # 193

Dear Bill,

IRISH BLESSINGS

May you always have work for your hands to do,
May your pockets hold always a coin or two,
May the sun shine bright on your window pane,
May the rainbow be certain to follow each rain,
May the hand of a friend always be near you,
And, may God fill your heart with gladness
to cheer you.

From your friend, John

Monday, August 30, 2010

Letter # 193

Dear Bill,

There was a time
When I could hit
The nail right on the head.
But the older I grow
The more likely I am
To hit my thumb
            instead.

—BOB CODER—

From your friend, John

Tuesday, August 31, 2010

Letter # 194

Dear Bill,

Today —
My bicycle ride
       started well,
I felt so fresh and agile.
      but as the hour
       passed along,
My agile turned to FRAGILE.

Lyn Keys Tutor
and
John Christian

From your friend, John

Wednesday, September 1, 2010

Letter #195

Dear Bill,

Why do we exercise faithfully
By walking several miles or more,
Yet we circle the parking lot
                        endlessly

Looking for a space
                close to the door?

From your friend, John

Thursday, September 2, 2010

Letter #196

Dear Bill,

JEREMIAH 30:17

" I will restore you to HEALTH
and HEAL your wounds;
declares the LORD, ..."

Bill, our prayer is that you will soon be
healed and whole.
Love John & Peggy

From your friend, John

Friday, September 3, 2010

Letter #197

Dear Bill,

When
a
piece
of
Heaven
" falls "
to
earth
" it
" becomes "
" a
garden

Isn't it great to
live in Callaway
Gardens? —Where
our dreams have
come
true!

From your friend, John

Saturday September 4, 2010

Letter #198

Dear Bill,

I have been driven
many times
upon my knees
by the
overwhelming conviction
that I had
nowhere else
to go.

ABRAHAM LINCOLN

From your friend, John

Sunday, September 5, 2010

Letter # 199

Dear Bill,

LIVE

in such a way
that if anyone
should speak
badly of you
no one
would believe it.

From your friend, John

Monday, September 6, 2010

Letter # 200

Dear Bill,

➡️ MOTTO TO LIVE BY

Life should not
be a journey to the grave
with the intention of arriving
safely
in an attractive and well preserved body,

BUT

rather to skid in sideways, chocolate
in one hand, latte in the other, body
thoroughly used up, totally worn-out and
screaming:

"WOO HOO, what a ride!

AUTHOR UNKNOWN

FROM
YOUR
FRIEND,
JOHN

Tuesday, September 7, 2010

Letter # 201

Dear Bill,

MOTHERS OF LITTLE BOYS
WORK FROM
SON UP
'TIL
SON DOWN!

From your friend,
John

Wednesday, September 8, 2010

Letter # 202

DEAR BILL,

WHERE THERE IS
GREAT LOVE
THERE ARE ALWAYS
Miracles

WILLA CATHER — AMERICAN AUTHOR

From your friend, John

P.S. Embrace and hold onto your
miracle today!

Thursday, September 9, 2010

Letter # 203

Dear Bill,

Psalm 28:7

The LORD is my strength
                    and shield;
My heart♥ trusts in Him,
                    and I am helped.
My heart♥ leaps for joy
and I will give thanks to Him in song.
                              Amen!

From your friend, John

Friday, September 10, 2010

Letter # 204

Dear Bill,

PHILIPPIANS 4:19

My GOD
will meet _all_ your needs
according to His
glorious riches
in
Christ Jesus.

From your friend, John

Saturday, September 11, 2010

Letter # 205

Dear Bill,

Theres one thing
I can't understand;
I've never understood it.
How can something disappear
From exactly where I put it?

— Sharon Dyer —

From your friend, John

Sunday, September 12, 2010

Letter # 206

Dear Bill,

<u>Prayer</u>

Forgive me, Lord, for the times I fail
To appreciate all You do.
I praise You now with humble heart
Filled with gratitude to you.

— Bessie L. Kennedy —

From your friend, John

Monday, September 13, 2010

Letter # 207

Dear Bill,

Making Choices

"One's philosophy is not best expressed in words.
It is expressed in the CHOICES one makes.
In the long run, we SHAPE our lives
and we SHAPE ourselves. The process
never ends. And the CHOICES we make
are ultimately our responsibility."

{ Eleanor
Roosevelt }

From your friend, John

Tuesday, September 14, 2010

Letter #208

Dear Bill,

We are children
of a living God,
and He not only walks with us,
but He honors us
by dwelling within us
and

CHANGING US FOREVER.

Thank
You
Lord Amen!

From your friend, John

Wednesday, September 15, 2010

Letter # 210

Dear Bill,

> " Whether you think you can,
> Or whether you think you can't,
> You're right. "
>
> HENRY FORD ~

From your friend, John

Thursday, September 16, 2010

Letter #211

Dear Bill,

FAITH

"...When God is seen
by faith's closest,
fullest eye
prayer creates
a history of wonders."

—EM BOUNDS—

From your friend, John

Friday, September 17, 2010

Letter # 212

Dear Bill,

Prayer

Yield! I will allow God to make out my "TO DO" list each day and my "PRAYER LIST" each day — because He (God) never gives us something to do, or to pray about that he doesn't see it through as He shows us the Way!

- John Christian -

From your friend, John

Saturday, September 18, 2010

Letter # 213

Dear Bill,

I've walked through the bloody stripes
That paid the price for me.
Healing is my portion
And my body is set free.
Never again will I say
That I am weak, or sick, or sore
Because I am completely healed
By the stripes that Jesus bore.

— From Freda Bower's Book: "Give me
40 Days for Healing."

"... by His stripes, I am healed!"
(1 Peter 2:24)

From your friend, John

Sunday, September 19, 2010

Letter #214

Dear Bill,

Sometimes people bug me,

I wish people would pay
more attentoin
to whath
they are doing.

—Author Unknown—

From your friend, John

Monday, September 20, 2010

Letter # 214

Dear Bill,

MIRACLE

DO NOT PRAY FOR EASY LIVES
    PRAY TO BE STRONGER MEN.
        DO NOT PRAY FOR TASKS
            EQUAL TO YOUR POWERS;
                PRAY FOR POWERS EQUAL TO YOUR TASKS.
                    THEN THE DOING OF YOUR WORK
                SHALL BE NO MIRACLE,
            BUT YOU SHALL BE A MIRACLE.
        EVERY DAY YOU SHALL WONDER AT YOURSELF,
    AT THE RICHNESS OF YOUR LIFE
WHICH HAS COME TO YOU
        BY THE GRACE OF GOD.

-PHILLIP BROOKS-

From your friend, John

Tuesday, September 21, 2010

Letter # 216

Dear Bill,

Walk in the Light.

There is a light where'er I go.
There is a splendor where I wait.
Though all around be desolate,
Warm on my eyes I feel a glow.

The fight is long, the triumph slow,
Yet shall my soul stand strong and straight,
There is a light where'er I go,
There is a splendor where I wait.

From your friend, John

Prayer & Praise: Lord because we
have accepted You — We are "children of light."
Amen!

Wednesday, September 22, 2010

Letter # 217

Dear Bill,

Cast Your Bread

There is a destiny
   that makes us brothers;
None goes his way alone.
All that we send
   into the lives of others
Comes back into our own ...

— Excerpt — Edwin Markham —

From your friend, John

Thursday, September 23, 2010

Letter # 218

Dear Bill,
   Here is one of my prayers this morning:

Good morning Lord!
   May your "Wellspring of Life" within me,
rise up, filling my body, soul, and spirit
with Divine Health. Not just for me, but
for all of my friends and family on my
prayer list. I (we) accept your Divine
Health — Your Wholeness — now we rejoice
that we are healed, we're free from pain.
   I pray in the name of Our Great Physician,
JESUS! Amen!

From your friend, John

Friday, September 24, 2010

Letter # 219

Dear Bill,

More people should learn
to tell their dollars
where to go
instead of asking them
where they went.
— Roger W. Babson —

From your friend, John

Saturday, September 25, 2010

Letter # 220

Dear Bill,

From Red Skelton's:
    "Recipe for the Perfect Marriage:

Two times a week we go to a nice
restaurant, have a little beverage, good
food and companionship. She goes on
Tuesdays, I go on Fridays.

From your friend, John

Sunday, September 26, 2010

Letter # 221

Dear Bill,

Another one — From Red Skelton's:

"Recipe for the Perfect Marriage"

My wife told me the car wasn't running well,
that there was water in the carburetor.
I asked her where the car was.
She told me, "In the lake".

From your friend, John

Monday, September 27, 2010

Letter # 222

Dear Bill,

WHAT ONE APPROVES,
    ANOTHER SCORNS,
AND THUS HIS NATURE
    EACH DISCLOSES;
ONE FINDS THE ROSE BUSH
        FULL OF THORNS,
THE OTHER FINDS IT
        FULL OF ROSES.

— SLIGHTLY MODIFIED, FROM ARTHUR GUITERMAN —

From your friend, John

Tuesday, September 28, 2010

Letter # 223

Dear Bill,

Cherish

Your visions;
Your ideals;
The music that stirs in your heart,
The beauty
that forms in your mind,
The loveliness
that drapes your purest thoughts...

If you
but remain true to them,
your world
will at last be built.

James Allen

From your friend, John

Wednesday, September 29, 2010

Letter # 224

Dear Bill and Glenda
A Prayer for you:

— JOY —

Psalm 16:11

You have made known to me
    the path of life,
You will fill me with Your Joy
    in Your presence,
With eternal pleasures
    at your right hand.
        Amen !

From your friend, John

Thursday, September 30, 2010

Letter # 225

Dear Bill,

Psalm 30:2

I called to You for help
and You healed me.

Amen

Bill, we continue to pray for healing and
peace, confidence, grace as you are being
healed.

From your friend, John

Friday, October 1, 2010

Letter #226

Dear Bill,

Definition of Shopping:

The Art
of buying things
you don't need
with money
you don't have
to impress people you don't even like

— "Sound Off" Columbus Ledger —

From your friend, John

Saturday, October 2, 2010

Letter # 227

Dear Bill,

<u>I Wish</u>

"I wish there was some wonderful place
In the land of "Beginning Again",
Where all our mistakes and
              all our heartaches
And all our poor selfish grief
Could be dropped like a shabby old
              coat at the door
And never be put on again."
              —Louise Tarkington—

From your friend, John

Sunday, October 3, 2010

Letter # 228

Dear Bill,

Micah 7:7

As for me,
I watch in hope for the Lord,
I wait for God my Savior;
My God will hear me.

From your friend, John

Monday, October 4, 2010

Letter # 229

Dear Bill

The most satisfying thing in life
is to have been able to give
a large part of oneself
to others.

—Pierre Teilhard de Chardin—

From your friend, John

Tuesday, October 5, 2010

Letter #230

Dear Bill,

Real letters from children to God:

Dear God. If you give me a genie lamp like Alladin, I will give you anything you want except my money
and my chess set. Ralph

Dear God. Please send Dennis Clark to a different summer camp this year.
Peter

From your friend, John

Wednesday, October 6, 2010

Letter # 231

Dear Bill,

Yesterday, I read in the newspaper:

It costs the tax payer:

1. 6 cents to make a penny,
   5 cents to make a dime, and
   10 cents to make a nickel.

Why are we doing this?
        It just doesn't make _cents_!

From your friend, John

Thursday, Oct 7, 2010

Letter # 232

Dear Bill,

On Thursday morning (early) March 5, 2009
I wrote this in my journal:

It is what <u>I do</u>, that changes my life,

<u>not</u> what I read about, think about,

or think would be nice to do.

— John Christian

From your friend, John

Dear Bill and Glenda, this morning we are heading for
Pennsylvania. I hope you enjoyed your trip to Florida. I
will pray for you daily <u>and</u> give you a stack of letters when we
return.
— John & Peggy Christian

Friday, October 8, 2010

Letter # 233

Dear Bill,

Time is but the stream
I go a-fishing in...

HENRY
DAVID
THOREAU

From your friend, John

Saturday, Oct 9, 2010

Letter # 234

Dear Bill,

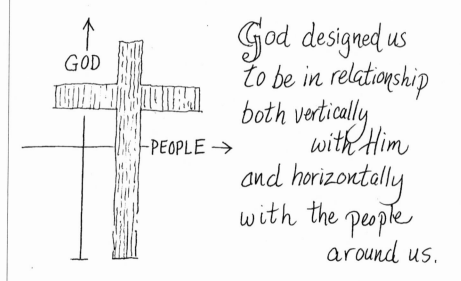

God designed us
to be in relationship
both vertically
with Him
and horizontally
with the people
around us.

From your friend, John

Sunday, October 10, 2010

Letter # 235

Dear Bill,

I must remember
   that everyone I meet
      is afraid of something
         loves something, and
            has lost something.

- Adapted from a quote by H. Jackson Brown -

From your friend, John

Monday, October 11, 2010

Letter # 236

Dear Bill,

My Home

My home
is my welcoming world,
my anchor,
the resting place
for my heart.

— Thomas
Kinkade

From your friend, John

Tuesday, October 12, 2010

Letter # 237

Dear Bill,

And this is our life...
To find tongues in trees,
Books in the running brooks
Sermons in stones,

And good in everything.

◄ WILLIAM SHAKESPEARE ►

From your friend, John

Wednesday, October 13, 2010

Letter # 238

Dear Bill,

Faith

THE WAY TO SEE

BY **FAITH**

IS TO SHUT THE EYE

OF **REASON**.

◄◗◖ BENJAMIN ◗◖►
FRANKLIN

From your friend, John

P.S. Let's continue to have faith
in your complete
and total healing. Amen!

Thursday, October 14, 2010

Letter # 239

Dear Bill,

Adversity

"There is one thing that we all have in common. That is — at some point in our life, we will face adversity. It is not a matter of if, but when. In my sixty three years on this earth, I have come to realize that the difference in our success or failure is not chance but choice. Because when adversity strikes, it's not what happens that will determine our destiny; it's _how we react_ to what happens." Mac Anderson

From your friend, John

Friday, October 15, 2010

Letter # 240

Dear Bill,

Greatness

IS

DETERMINED

BY

Service

Martin
Luther
King

From your friend, John

Saturday, October 16, 2010

Letter # 241

Dear Bill,

Someone
once said
that the secret
of genius
is to carry
the spirit of the child
into old age.

Author Unknown

From your friend, John

Sunday, October 17, 2010

Letter # 242

Dear Bill,

Have you ever felt this way?

I'm so far behind ☆ ☆ ☆
            I thought I was first!

AUTHOR
UNKNOWN

From your friend, John

Monday, October 18, 2010

Letter # 243

Dear Bill, In order to keep down the clutter and, because your Doctor's report was so encouraging last week, I will deliver a letter just once a week. Your healing is taking place, if not complete already and prayers still go up daily!

For this week :

"But that brings us to
    A paradox, A mystery
    Of time and eternity.

Simply put:
    We can aim for the eternal,
    But we can only act
        In the Present
            Moment."

    —Thomas Kinkade, "Simpler Times"—

From your friend, John

Monday October 25, 2010

Letter # 244

Dear Bill & Glenda

Life

Life is measured
by the number of things
we are alive to.

— MALTBIE D. BABCOCK —

My prayer for each of you today is that
you have life and have it abundantly!

From your friend, John

Monday, November 1, 2010

Letter # 245

Dear Bill,

I thank and praise God for His miraculous healing and provision for you!

The
real
voyage
of
discovery
consists
not in
seeking
new
landscapes, but
in
having
new
eyes. — Marcel Proust —

From your friend, John

Monday, November 8, 2010

Letter # 246

~~He~~ ~~A~~lone

He alone
stretches out the heavens
and treads on the waves
of the sea.

He is
the maker of the Bear and Orion,
the Pleiades and the
constellations of the south

He performs
wonders that cannot be fathomed
Miracles
that cannot be numbered.

FROM
THE BOOK OF JOB

He heals your cancer!

From your friend, John

Monday, November 15, 2010

Letter # 247

Dear Bill,

On the Path

I will recognize my own Path
when I come upon it,
Because I will suddenly have all
of the
ENERGY
and
IMAGINATION
I will ever need.

From your friend, John

Jerry
Gillies

Monday, November 22, 2010

Letter # 248

Dear Bill,

A special prayer for
health and healing:

Never a weakness that
He does not feel,
Never a sickness that
He cannot heal,
Never a sorrow that
He does not share,
Moment by moment
I'm under His care.
— DANIEL WHITTLE —

From your friend, John

Monday, November 29, 2010

Letter # 249

Dear Bill,

When the trials of this life
        make you weary,
And your troubles
        seem too much to bear,
There's a wonderful
        solace and comfort,
In the silent
        Communion of prayer.

-AUTHOR UNKNOWN-

From your friend, John

God bless you and may your healing be complete!

Monday, December 6, 2010

Letter # 250

Dear Bill,

    I know, <u>beyond a shadow of doubt</u> that God has healed me from some several serious diseases. Here is a scripture I often quote out loud that brings healing:

    Bless the Lord, O my soul;
        and all that is within me bless His Holy name.
    Bless the Lord, O my soul;
        and forget not all His benefits.
    Who forgiveth all thine iniquities;
    Who <u>healeth</u> <u>all</u> thy diseases.

                — PSALM 103: 1-3 —

There is <u>nothing</u> from heaven withheld from the one whose mouth is filled with praise for the Provider. (God) <u>Amen</u>!

                -Charles G. Finney

From your friend, John

Monday, December 13, 2010

Letter # 251

Dear Bill and Glenda

— Praying for both of you this morning!

Sweet Hour of Prayer

PRAYER

Sweet hour of prayer, sweet hour of prayer,
That calls me from a world of care,
And bids me at my Father's throne,
Make all my wants and wishes known.
In seasons of distress and grief,
My soul has often found relief,
And oft escaped the tempter's snare,
By thy return, sweet hour of prayer.

Sweet hour of prayer, sweet hour of prayer,
Thy wings shall my petition bear
To Him, who truth and faithfulness
Engage the waiting soul to bless:
And since He bids me seek His face,
Believe His Word and trust His Grace,
I'll cast on Him my every care,
And wait for thee, sweet hour of prayer.

— W. W. WALFORD —

From your friend, John

Monday, December 20, 2010

Letter # 252

Dear Bill,

FAITH

IS LIKE RADAR

THAT SEES

THROUGH THE FOG —

THE REALITY

OF THINGS AT A DISTANCE

THAT THE HUMAN EYE CANNOT SEE.

— CORRIE TEN BOOM —

~ PRAYERS FOR YOU THIS MORNING ~

From your friend, John

Monday, December 27, 2010

Letter # 253

Dear Bill

What a great Christmas Dinner we had!
What a wonderful White Christmas evening
we enjoyed!

an obedient FAITH must be lived out
step by step,
day by day.
we need new faith for each new day.
To enjoy the life God intends for us,
we must Daily lay everything
down and let everything go in
SURRENDER TO HIM.
Once we release everything --- we
receive more than we can ever imagine!

From your friend, John

Adapted from Dr. Rick Warren,
author: "The Purpose
Driven Life"

Monday January 3, 2011

Letter # 254

Dear Bill and Glenda

January, the month of new beginnings...
    and wonderful possibilities
        and
        healing
        and
    wholeness!

Bill, Gods precious Holy Spirit dwells in
You --- their is _no sickness_ in God, He
is perfectly healthy; therefore since God is
in You --- there is nothing but good health
in You. Continue to accept it _and_ continue to
eat your asparagus juice too. By the way
on Jan 1st (twice a day) I have 4 TBSP's myself
each morning and each evening. It's not so bad!

From your friend, John

Monday, January 10, 2011

Letter # 255

Dear Bill,
    I am thankful everyday for the healing taking place in your life right now. My prayer is that the prognosis will continue to improve until you are completely healed and whole! Amen!
Gratitude is one of the Key elements in the process of healing.

Gratitude
        unlocks the fullness of life.
        It turns what we have
        into enough and more.
        It turns denial into acceptance,
        chaos to order, confusion to clarity.
        It can turn a meal into a feast,
        A house into a home,   — by
        A stranger into a friend.   Melody
                                                Beattie —
Gratitude makes sense of our past,
    Brings peace for today, and creates a
                        Vision
                            for tomorrow.

From, your
    friend
        John

Monday, January 17, 2011

Letter # 256

Dear Bill,

DREAMS...

If one advances
   confidently in the direction
of his dreams,
   and endeavors to live the life
which he has imagined,
   He will meet with a success
unexpected in common hours.

—Henry
David
Thoreau—

I hope you and Glenda have
   a great day!

From your friend, John

Monday, January 24, 2011

Letter # 257

Dear Bill,

The Holy Spirit

God is in me
as the sun
is in the
fragrance
and color
of a flower.

— Helen Keller —

From your friend, John

P.S. Prayer for Today: Lord, <u>this day</u> I ask You to enlarr
my life beyond what I can ima

Monday, January 31, 2011

Letter # 258

Dear Bill,

What you think
  might be the
    end of the road
      is often just
        the bend in the road.

-AUTHOR UNKNOWN-

From your friend, John

PS Our prayer for You and Glenda is that this is just a bend in the road ---that the _new_ medication _and_ prayers will bring strength and _new_ hope. God bless! Love John & Peggy

Monday, February 7, 2011

Letter # 259

<u>If</u>

If the sight of the blue skies
    fills you with joy
If a blade of grass springing up
    in the fields
    has power to move you
If the simple things of nature
    have a message
    that you understand,

<u>Rejoice</u> for your soul is alive!

<u>Bill</u> — ym and Glenda have always enjoyed
many beautiful things together
and <u>always</u> will.
    PRAYING FOR YOU!

From your friend, John

<u>Valentine's Day</u> Monday, February 14, 2011

Letter # 260

Dear Bill,

<u>HOME SONG</u>

EVERY HOUSE
     WHERE LOVE ABIDES
AND FRIENDSHIP
     IS A GUEST,
IS SURELY HOME,
     AND HOME SWEET HOME;
FOR THERE THE HEART ♥
     CAN REST.

HENRY
VAN
DYKE

From your friend, John

— PRAYING FOR YOU TODAY! —

Monday, February 20, 2011

Letter # 261

Dear Bill and Glenda
    May God continue to be with you both
today providing peace, strength, and courage.
    This morning early, before daylight, I
walked out on the front porch as I often do.
I raised my arms to the beautiful heavens, the
stars were out and a 3/4 moon was glowing. It
was cold but refreshing. I thanked God for
one more day on this earth — even though I
know I will live forever. This special morning
reminded me of this quote:
        Look at the STARS! Look,
            look up at the skies!
        Oh look at all the fire-folk
                sitting in the air!
        The bright burroughs,
                the circle-citadels there.
                                    by Gerald
God bless   Manley
        you both!   Hopkins
    From your friend, John

Monday, February 28, 2011

Letter # 262

Dear Bill,

Prayer

Lord, may I continue to say,
a deep passionate **YES**
to the things
in life

that really matter and **NO!**
to those that don't, and
may Your peace settle into my soul
like golden sunlight
sifting to a forest floor.

—Loosely adapted from
a quote by artist,
Thomas Kinkade—

From your friend,
John

Monday, March 7, 2011

Letter # 263

Dear Bill, Even though we at times go through
a terrible, difficult struggle, there are
still things around us that remain constant
and sure:

The Beauty Around Us

A thing of beauty
        is a joy forever;
It's loveliness increases;
It will never pass
        into nothingness;
But still will keep
        a bower of quiet for us,
And a sleep
    Full of sweet dreams
    And health
        And quiet breathing.
                        John
                        Keats

Praying for you today!

Your friend, John

Wednesday, March 16, 2011

Letter #264

My dear friend,

I've searched through old journals, books of poetry, papers and notes looking for appropriate, effective words of inspiration, comfort, and courage. I found many, and they were good, but none were quite right for the emotions I feel now. Yesterdays report on the MRI didn't look good and the news was heart-breaking. I can't imagine how you feel right now or what you're going through — because, as much as we might try, we really can't walk in another's shoes. So, again, this morning in prayer for You and others, I asked God to show me some words. He led me to this:

He said Cling to Verse #13 (Matt 6:13) of the Lord's Prayer:

FOR THINE IS THE KINGDOM, AND THE POWER,
AND THE GLORY, FOREVER. AMEN. , and

Verse #6 of the 23rd Psalm:
...AND I WILL DWELL IN THE HOUSE OF THE LORD FOREVER.

Bill I believe we are dwelling in HIS HOUSE (THE HOUSE OF THE LORD) right now, because as Christians we never die, we just walk through the door into Heaven.

Nothing, anywhere, says it so clearly and as perfectly as
                God's Word.
             Praying for You!
With love, from your friend, John

Monday, March 21, 2011

Letter # 265

Dear Bill,

As much as you've enjoyed the mountains of the west, northwest, and Alaska, I hope you can relate to this short excerpt from "The Spell of the Yukon:

I've stood in some mighty-mouthed hollow
    That's plumb-full of hush to the brim;
I've watched the big, husky sun wallow
    In crimson and gold, and grow dim,
Till the moon set the pearly peaks gleaming,
    And the stars tumbled out, neck and crop;
And I've thought that I surely was dreaming,
    With the peace o' the world piled on top.

From: "The Spell of the Yukon" by Robert W. Service

From your friend, John

Monday, March 28, 2011

Letter #266

Dear Bill,   I thought you might enjoy this:

Theyre back! Those wonderful Church Bulletins! Thank God for church ladies with typewriters and word processors. These sentences (with their bloopers) actually appeared in church bulletins or were announced in church services:

- In church today, smile as you meet new people, and don't forget to say Hell to even those who don't seem to care about you.

- The sermon this morning: "Jesus Walks on Water." The sermon tonight: "Searching for Jesus."

- Next Thursday there will be tryouts for the choir. They need all the help they can get.

- Irving Benson and Jessie Carter were married on Oct 24 in the church. So ends a friendship that began in their early school days.

- A bean supper will be held on Tuesday evening in the Fellowship Hall. Music will follow.

- The Boy Scouts are saving aluminum cans, bottles, and other items to be recycled. Proceeds will be used to cripple children.

- Pot luck supper, Sunday at 5:00pm - prayer and medication will follow.

From your friend John

Praying for You!

Monday, April 4, 2011

Letter # 267

Dear Bill, Here are 7 more:

- The ladies of the church have cast off clothing of every kind. They may be seen in the basement on Friday afternoon.

- This evening at 7 pm there will be a hymn singing in the park across from the church. Bring a blanket and and come prepared to sin.

- Ladies Bible Study will be held Thursday morning at 10:00am. All ladies are invited to lunch when the BS is done.

- The pastor would appreciate it if the ladies of the congregation would lend him their electric girdles for the pancake breakfast Saturday morning.

- LOW SELF ESTEEM SUPPORT GROUP will meet Thursday at 7 PM. Please use the back door.

- The 8th graders will present Shakespeare's Hamlet in the church basement Fri at 7:00pm. The public is invited to attend this tragedy. _And finally,_

- Weight Watchers will meet at 7:00pm at the 1st Presbyterian Church. Please use the large double doors at the side of the building.

From your friend, John   May God bless You, Glenda and Your Family in a very special way today!

Monday, April 11, 2011

Letter #268

Dear Bill,
    I miss the times that we worked together as volunteers in Callaway Gardens. We had some great times _and_ we enjoyed the fried chicken in the EC (Employees _Cafeteria_).
    There have been a few times in my life when I have been very sick. As I lay in bed suffering, I try to visualize in my mind's eye a beautiful place to retreat to — and it usually is a garden. Probably Callaway Gardens. With my eyes closed, I hold out my hand and say, "Take it Lord, lead me through the garden" — and He does. We walk down a gravel covered pathway, with mist slowly rising, in the twilight. I see the outlines and perfect symmetry of flowering trees, scent of pine, cascading ferns, a brook with small waterfalls. The pathway leads to a beautifully filtered warm glow of light — a perfect place — I feel it is leading me HOME.
    I have always known that _in the garden_, when I let Him lead — He walks with me and He talks with me, and tells me that I am His own. And that is enough!
                      Amen!

From your friend, John

— Praying for You, Glenda, and Your family daily! —

Monday, April 18, 2011

Letter # 269

Dear Bill,

from the Bay Psalm Book

The Lord to me a shepherd is,
    want therefore shall not I:
He in the folds of tender grass,
    doth cause me down to lie:
To waters calm me gently leads
    restore my soul doth He:
He doth in paths of righteousness
    for His name's sake lead me
Yea though in valley of death's shade
    I walk, non ill I fear:
Because thou art with me, thy rod,
    and staff my comfort are.
For me a table thou hast spread,
    in presence of my foes:
Thou dost annoint my head with oil;
    my cup it overflows.
Good ness and mercy surely shall
    all my days follow me:
And in the Lord's House I shall dwell
    so long as days shall be.

From your friend John

☀ LOVE & PRAYERS
DAILY
FOR BILL, GLENDA
AND FAMILY

John Christian

John Christian was born in Goldsboro, North Carolina. He received an M.S. degree in Commercial Art from Louisiana Tech University, Ruston, Louisiana, and an M.S. degree from Troy State University, Troy, Alabama. John spent thirty years as an Air Force Officer. The last ten years he was a Lieutenant Colonel and Squadron Commander assigned to Air Force Special Operations Command, Eglin Air Force Base, Florida. He also served for ten years as a Faculty Member and Director of Media Services, Charleston Southern University, Charleston, South Carolina.

John and his wife, Peggy, have three grown children and eight grandchildren. After retirement from the Air Force, John worked as an artist, specializing in   watercolor painting and pen and ink drawings. He has painted murals on buildings in Florida and recently, on a building in Georgia. He has also taught drawing classes for children.

John and Peggy live at Longleaf in Callaway Gardens, Pine Mountain, Georgia. He continues to do artwork and is active in numerous church and community projects. His greatest delight is spending time with Peggy, his children, grandchildren, and friends.